meet the family
my sister

by Mary Auld

W
FRANKLIN WATTS
LONDON·SYDNEY

This is Sally and her sister Kate, with their mum and dad. Sally is three years younger than Kate.

Brian's sister is much older than him. Sometimes she helps their mum look after him.

Briony and Louise are identical twins. Only their mum and dad can tell which sister is which.

Anne has a new
baby sister, Lucy.
Lucy has a different
mum from Anne,
so she's her
half-sister.

Nicky and Ruby are best friends – and step-sisters. They have different parents, but now Ruby's dad is married to Nicky's mum.

Kevin and his sister go to the same school but are in different classes.

Mary's sister is in a
football team.

Miguel's sister paints
beautiful pictures.
Sometimes she lets
Miguel help.

Lizzie teases her sister.

Gareth makes his sister giggle.

Leo and his sister play
cards together.

Mel and her sisters
like putting on shows
for their parents.

This is Nina
with her mum
and her mum's
sister – Nina's
Auntie Janet.

Do you have a sister?
What's she like?

Family words

Here are some words people use when talking
about their sister or family.

Names for children:
Sister, Brother; Daughter, Son.

Names for parents:
Father, Daddy, Dad, Pa;
Mother, Mummy, Mum, Ma.

Names of other relatives:
Grandchildren; Grandparents;
Grandmother, Granny, Grandma;
Grandfather, Grandad, Grandpa;
Uncle; Aunt, Auntie; Nephew; Niece.

If we put the word 'Step' in front of a relative's name, it means
that we are related to them by marriage but not by birth.

If we put the word 'Half' in front of our brother or sister,
it means that one of our parents is the same
and the other is different.

A family tree

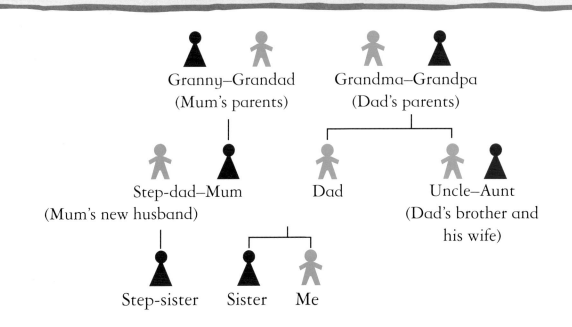

Granny–Grandad
(Mum's parents)

Grandma–Grandpa
(Dad's parents)

Step-dad–Mum
(Mum's new husband)

Dad

Uncle–Aunt
(Dad's brother and
his wife)

Step-sister

Sister

Me

You can show how you are related to all your family on a plan like this one. It is called a family tree. Every family tree is different. Try drawing your own.

First published in 2003 by Franklin Watts,
96 Leonard Street, London EC2A 4XD

Franklin Watts Australia
45-51 Huntley Street, Alexandria, NSW 2015

Copyright © Franklin Watts 2003

Series editor: Rachel Cooke
Art director: Jonathan Hair
Design: Andrew Crowson

A CIP catalogue record for this book
is available from the British Library.

ISBN 0 7496 5115 6

Printed in Hong Kong/China

Acknowledgements:
Paul Baldesare/Photofusion: 13. Bruce
Berman/Corbis: front cover main, 22.
www.johnbirdsall.co.uk: front cover centre
below, 2, 5. Dex Images Inc/Corbis: 1, 14.
Paul Doyle/Photofusion: 16. Jon Feingersch/
Corbis: 12. Carlos Goldin/Corbis: front cover
centre above. Sally Greenhill, Sally & Richard
Greenhill: 6, 11, 20-21. Ronnie Kauffman/

Corbis: 8-9. Roy McMahon/Corbis: 18. Jose
Luis Pelaez/Corbis: front cover centre top.
George Shelley/Corbis: front cover bottom.
Ariel Skelley/Corbis: front cover centre. Paula
Solloway/Format: 17. Mo Wilson/Format: 19.

Whilst every attempt has been made to clear
copyright should there be any inadvertent
omission please apply in the first instance to
the publisher regarding rectification.

Please note that some of the pictures in this book have been posed by models.